FIONA'S POEMS

by

MALCOLM COX

CW00517255

First Edition
Interesting Place
Axbridge Somerset
2001

Copyright © Malcolm Cox and Fiona Napier-Bell

Original photowork and cover design by Malcolm Cox

CONTENTS

A first volume of poems
to, and about Fiona,
written by Malcolm Cox.

If less is more, Peter Pan, then there's no end to me!

Tinka Bell

ISBN 0 9533982 2 6
INTERESTING PLACE 2001

En bon point!

Come on Malc, don't mess,
what d'you really reckon to this dress?
Don't spare my feelings,
send 'em reeling, if that's what honesty dictates!
Does it make my bum look huge,
or underestimate my boobs?

You can see right through the skirt?
I wear a thong, that won't hurt!
And my stomach? Tam, the bitch's
said it strains it at the stitch's!

Miss Bell, Miss Bell!
Relax Miss Bell!
No need for stress,
you rhyme so well.
Your ample stanzas are a pure poetic vision,
curving, as they do, from form to rhythm.
I'm certain that these graces rude
are no mere metric interlude!

Miss Bell,
Miss Bell, you little Tinka!
Through the village dusk
your flight's
a fiery beacon of delights.
Twinkling through each gay weekending,
petering the willing Pans,
sending-off offended Wendys wending!
There's more than one
who'd care to bust
your generous supplies
of Pixie Dust!!

But you're a rider, and a shot.
You swim and dance, you sing, the lot!
Your skill on horseback, in the season,
is legend in the Western Region.
No chance of Wendy catching you.
Your Dad is rich,
your blood is blue!

I hear from Neverland, second right,
especially on a friday night,
that Hook and Smee
have joined the band
of Lost Boys waiting on the sand!

I clearly see you can't be caught,
but if I tell you I believe,
and clap,
do you come?
Now there's a thought!!

∎

If I loved you.

If <u>I</u>
   loved you,
then I would love
the smell of you,
the taste, the touch,
the woman in the girl of you,
the say, the hear,
the tell of you.
<u>If</u>
I loved you.

If <u>I</u>
   loved you,
then I would love
the spark of you,
the curl, the laugh,
the breathing in the dark of you,
the curve, the sleep,
the shadows in the deep of you,
the how of you,
the why of you,
the was, the now,
the shall of you.
<u>If</u>
I loved you.

■

Quite different!

She is very young.
I am not.
She asked for a poem.
I made her two.

I keep them,
she told me,
in my most private, parent-proof box,
under lock and key,
together with my cigarettes,
my condoms and my dodgy photos!

Strange companions for poetry, I thought,
although the point of it
did not escape me.

But what if, I asked,
I want to publish them,
in a book,
for the World to read?

Oh, that's OK, she readily agreed,
as long as you tell the World
that you made them for me.

But,
by my bed,
she said,
a poem
would be
quite different!!

■

It occurred to me.

It occurred to me
that
the really tantalising thing
is that
sometimes,
being with you
is like being half of a really good couple.
You know,
the kind of couple you always imagined being
but never quite managed to be!

Don't get me wrong,
I'm not looking for a partner,
and would decline <u>any</u> sensible offer.

I <u>know</u> the various fates of romantic love.
I have sown, and harvested the seeds of its destruction.
I have seen its bones
laid bleached
upon the stoney beach of marital familiarity.
<u>And</u> shielded my eyes
as it imploded
into a thousand glassy fragments.
I've done both!

I also know the value
of falling in love
with someone
who is, in principle, unattainable.
Someone met at a crossroads
who is travelling a different journey.
I know the value of its passing warmth!

You,
the Young Heiress,
off to finishing-school this autumn.
One of the hottest,
most sought-after
and most 'drop-dead-gorgeous' girls in the County,
I would guess.

Me,
definitely not young,
but beautiful,
and rather special.
Mother, Father,
rider,
and is it on a road to successful authorship?

But,
when I'm with you,
that passionate yearning,
so deeply and so poignantly insatiable
whatever the age and circumstance,
undeniably
and seductively
beckons.

It tells me,
when I look at you,
the answer to the philosopher's question:
The evolutionary function
served by the delightfully neurotic state
of 'being in love'
is simply
'Rocket Fuel'!

Commitment of that sort,
voluntarily entertained,
is one of life's cliffs.
And without Rocket Fuel,
no one,
absolutely no one,
is going to make that leap,
are they?

When I look at you,
therefore,
the words of the old song
come back to me
to say:
'But what the hell,
I'd take the chance with you,
My Darling Girl!'

And so it is
that sometimes,
after dinner,
we sit
facing each other across the long kitchen table
among the dirty crocks,
half empty wineglasses,
half full coffee cups.

My kids off in the sitting -room,
watching tele beside the fire
while dusk reclaims the Moor,
beyond the yard,
outside the door.

And while the smoke from your cigarette
draws gently up towards the light,
in silence I gaze at you,
with your deep, golden curls
which challenge every poetic cliché I ever knew,
and you gaze at me,
and smile,
and sometimes
we kiss . . . . .

■

Crumbs!

Crumbs!
I seem to have breathed you into every part of me!
My scalp,
my skin,
my tummy and my loins
(especially loins)
are all aglow with you!

Whenever you appear,
they all curl up and grin,
and call out:
Hello, my Darling!

Shush!
There it goes.
Listen quietly
and you'll hear my toes!

■

All the power is in the bum!

Well,
as to that,
I would say,
it is a secret
shared
unspoken.

If observed,
you will
most likely
find us grinning conspiratorially.

From beneath eyebrows
lowered in censure of your prurient interest,
we will inform you
that:

We weren't doing what you think we were doing!
We were, in fact,
discussing the ideal conformation
of a champion show-jumping pony.
The hocks are under
and all the power
is in the bum!

■

Like a cat!

She comes and goes like a cat,
my teenager.

Away so long
that the milk
in the saucer
is yoghurt,
and you assume
she's grown a home
on another hearthrug.

Then,
when you least expect it,
she's miaowing at the kitchen door
and I'm searching the fridge
for fresh cream!

One moment
she's on the keys of my typewriter
claiming my attention.
Then she's gone again.

Once in a while,
as they do,
she turns up
purring and snuggling,
at bedtime.

■

Strands.

It wasn't so much
that you came and knocked at my emotional door.
You had your own key.
You just let yourself in.

There's not many can do that,
and of those who can,
not many that I'd entertain.

I could, therefore,
have tipped you out,
back on to the doorstep, as it were.
But you entered with such panache.
I admired that,
and let you stay.

In due course
I adopted you,
as you asked.
Comfort was needed and I was giving.
That was OK.
I enjoyed that.
Me as Mum,
you as My Girl!

And somewhere amid the sitting and the talking,
as time went along,
we became friends,
mates,
mutual confidantes.

Then it turned sparky!
There were, for instance,
the dresses, on a Friday night,
as you prepared to do the wolving of the world.
You'd come to me,
at my typewriter,
you'd twirl, and ask me: Does this pull?
And to my surprise,
I saw you really cared
whether or not I was
(I was, of course. Who could fail to be?).

And the poetry:
You raided the English Modern Anthology,
for romance, for love.
You brought it to me,
and asked me to write you
… something?

Despite this slippery slope,
I suppose I might have remained unlaunched,
but one day,
in trial and tribulation
you came to me,
and there it was,
proximity!

And so,
quite suddenly really,
it was not just all the pieces,
the affection, friendship,
the attraction and the sparks that mattered.
Everything mattered,
most poignantly!

Why did you want me to fall in love with you?
Or is it that we always do,
being children at heart?

I <u>have</u> wondered
if I feign false innocence,
if I really saw it slide in beside you,
that year and more ago,
if it was not merely
            my door-key that you carried?

But either way,
I guess,
I would have let you stay.
I'd seen you grow,
and already cared.

But you do know
what I've bought, along with this,
don't you,
in letting it come this far?

One inevitably does.
It's loneliness!

■

Stormlight.

Sweet,
the smell of your breath
in the rain-rimmed darkness.

Soft,
the rise of your hip
drawn by fitful stormlight.

Deep,
the mumbled shadows of your growing-years
interwoven with the distant thunder.

Warm,
the sleeping curves of us,
tide-swept by cool night air.

Unhurried
the gentle rattle of the open casement.

Storm-tossed,
your golden curls
strewn darkly on my pillow.

God Almighty!
I could drown
in your sweet-breathing proximity!
The Lone Mariner
encountered a storm,
and is thought
to be lost
at sea!

■

Not often!

Curled up on my hearthrug
in front of the fire,
cuddling a crumpled duvet,
your hair spread like sea-fern
in an ebbing tide.

The childlike peace of you
belies the million and one
  teenage excitements which have brought you here
to sleep
this rainy mid-summer afternoon.

Not often do I want
to freeze-frame forever,
to keep you here
just as you are
for me!

■

What is it?

What is it?
What is it that touches me,
that diffidently holds my arm,
restrains me as I turn towards the door?

I held you,
now you sleep?

I switched off your lamp.

I kissed you,
the gentlest brushing of your brow,
most tenderly!

You murmured,
I replied.
No words, just the music of our breath.

I combed your falling curls
carefully from your face,
softly through my fingers,
to rest upon the pillow?

What is it?

I turn back
towards you,
peaceful now in the night-glow from your window.

I realise.
I smile.

It's only love that holds me,
only love!

■

How do you do that?

How do you do that?
Leave a clear, sky-blue hole
          exactly the shape and size of you
when you go?

How do you do it?
How do you move so fast?
One moment you, and then this space!

If we could anticipate,
we might 'count-down',
add our own semblance of magic to the process.
As it is, you lift away unannounced,
not so much a rocket at take off,
which are, initially at any rate,
agonisingly slow inverted volcanoes of hope,
but flashing blue,
incandescent,
ionising our atomic sensibilities,
bequeathing
a crackle of subsiding electrons.

Were it not for the rim,
slightly charred by the sudden discharge of your energy,
that space might be invisible,
imaginary.

But we see it,
and watch,
fascinated into pin-dropping silence
as the syrupy droplets of our psychological ether
slowly occupy your absence,
until someone speaks,
says:
'That was Fi!'

The eightieth letter.

Malc, I'm coming home, she cried,
her voice cracked by tears, and a bar or two of missing signal.
You don't know what this means to me . . . . . . !

Oh Love, I do, I called, crying too.
I'm so glad for you!

Boarding school,
so strangely British.
Seventy-nine days,
and seventy-nine letters
(I want one <u>every</u> day, she said.
Tell me that life goes on!).

I had wanted it to work for her
(although it was not of my doing).
Knew it would read incomparably on her CV.
Knew that she would meet the 'right' people,
one or two of whom would also be nice,
and she did!

But seventy-nine days
was all that she, and they could manage,
separated, as she was,
from the limb of her life.

Seventy-nine days in which,
I somehow felt,
they had failed to try.

I would not have lost her,
had I been House Parent.
I would have loved her,
but then I would have been home?

She tried!
Seventy-nine days
is a good try.
She proved her strength,
if at times in contrary ways.
But somehow I felt
that they,
older and supposedly wiser,
had not.
And now the breaking of it
broke us both
in tears.

Seventy-nine letters,
missing her and loving her,
wrote themselves
and were prepared
to be six hundred.

But now,
suddenly,
the eightieth letter,
its news and gossip gleanings hovering above the page,
its home-spun philosophies caught in mid-flight,
is no longer needed.

She will reconnect,
will see,
and hear for herself
all the small, dear things.

She is coming home!

■

Why me, why here, why now?

Black winter evening.
The tyres spray loose gravel
as I sweep the car around between cropped verges
and down into the small car park.

I am bemused.
The little Chef,
picked out by its thin red neon,
seems surreal.

I switch my window down
in an attempt to reconnect.

I am distracted
by the stream of rush-hour headlights
probing the scything rain along the motorway.
I am disconcerted by the hooligan wind
which bullies invisible trees into hissing anguish
and scatters scared leaves.

Why me, why here, why now?
What on earth am I doing here,
on this night,
at this point in my life,
in a car park
on the edge of a strange Devon village,
in a tight valley
snug with the ghosts of old orchards?

And then,
quite suddenly,
you detach yourself from the sheltering porchway
and run through the rain to meet the car.

It is your hand which operates the door-lock.
It is you wet-dogging in beside me.
You grin,
you shake your hair
and rain sparkles us.

Lights begin to shift,
sounds retune
and things make sense again.

I see exactly why my life
conspired to bring me here,
to this unknown place
at the edge of the world,
to this winter-dark doorway in the wind and rain.
It was simply,
and inexorably because
this was when,
and where you would be!

■

Schoolzout!

So many kids!
Such shapes and sizes,
ages!
A blizzard of children
released by the final bell of the day.

Smart, middle-class children,
chasing one another in the wind,
blown between antique, red-brick buildings,
securely middle-England.

The Autumn Gale sweeps them,
flying leaves,
to cars,
parents,
nannies
and school buses.
Little, unconfident ones;
large, blond and wavey, Rugby-playing ones.
The chic,
the stoned,
the bright and the phazed,
swot, nerd and tarty!

I wait in my car,
patiently bemused.
No problem of identification for me.
Mine
is the beautiful one!

■

Nearest and dearest.

The Millennium - 00/00/00
No-time.

Having, in the end,
no defence against such occasions,
I fled,
with four children who had no invitations,
to seek refuge
among the crowds on The Hoe.

It was all quite well done.
The bands were funky,
the fair-grounds bright and brittle with noise and movement,
and the burger-vans hot and busy.

At thirty minutes before no-time,
three of us took shelter from the sea-fret
within the northern arms of the war memorial,
where we watched the lights of the city below
dye the undersides of the flying clouds
unearthly amber
and lazers dance green among the buildings and the rain.

From the discordant clamour above us,
I guessed that thirty-four thousand,
nine hundred and ninety-nine other people
were seeking refuge
just as I.

Fionn, Robyn and I,
in the arms of the War Memorial,
grateful for the cover
          provided by so many dead
in that closing century,
sipping our flask-tea,
eating our chocolate,
and waiting
for no-time to arrive.

Out there,
in the throng rimming the amphitheatre,
I knew that Merin and Leanne
would be saved
by the wattage
of the numbing music.

At ten to no-time,
we left our nest,
to immerse ourselves in anonymity,
climbed the muddied slope,
a carpet of beer-cans and bottles underfoot,
towards the lighthouse,
until the pack closed around us
and we could move no further.
We waited . . . .

As we stood there,
tired, dazed,
and drunk on the incomprehensible cocktail of sound,
awaiting the nothing
which everyone had gathered to do
                    at the turning of no-time,
my thoughts were seized towards my 'nearest and dearest',
and as the seconds
ticked more and more slowly,
preparing for the stop,
I, almost idly,
                    wondered who these people might turn out to be.

Drawn against the moment,
the list began to assemble itself
in wilful independency.
First wife Lyn,
although that was not her name when she was,
came filing through the ruck.
Then children crowded in;
Phill, and Jo,
Fionn and Dear Robs
(of all that list the only ones by my side),
and Merin, my grumpy-love,
up ahead somewhere in the chaos.
My old friends Liz and Dave,
counties away in the Mid-West.
My cousin Jean,
just over the border in Cornwall,
and El,
but indistinct,
as if doubtful of her welcome.
Perhaps the strangest thing
was those who did not come
to share my no-time.

But as the air rocked and shook,
finally,
with no-time and the first salvo of fireworks,
as I was forcibly tongue-snogged
        by a serial-female of the crowd,
and as the rending of zero-time took reality apart,
I realised that I had always known
who would be at the top of that list.
You, Fi,
the one I really wanted beside me,
under my arm within the group,
strange, young and headstrong,
fused to a couple on the night of no-time.
That was what I really wanted
that was my anchor,
as time stood
perilously poised!

■

This is a woman.

I have never worshipped the gregarious sun,
seeking rather
(it seems)
a solace of moon-silvered waters,
carving my particular messages
upon the sands of slowly ebbing tides.

But now,
at last,
as chance runs,
I am caught-out by that unifying brilliance,
called upon to pay the price of my preoccupation,
exposed upon life's open ground.

Both manned,
and undone by its revealing magic,
I find myself
not poet half enough.

It was you, of course,
in case you wondered,
slim-hipped and fast,
summer glowing from every pore,
gold shouldered beneath your golden curls.

The July sun,
that day,
from its inscrutable blue heaven,
who could have chosen
to bring birth, or death,
chose instead
to sing a shining, golden-silver sheen
upon the down which grows between your breasts,
chose to say:
This is a woman;
please join me in celebration of that fact!

■

Remember.

I would like you to remember,
remember the day,
remember that it was autumn
and that you were seventeen.
Remember that
the shining air carried a frosty edge.

A snuggling, cosy sort of day,
its afternoon smile
broken into laughter,
much like our own.

Remember that the old city,
snug itself within its circling walls,
was crowded with shoppers,
and lives
who seemed that day so amiably disposed.

Remember you,
with your grey overcoat
buttoned to the neck
and your hat pulled down over your ears,
saying:
I can't possibly look sexy like this!

You,
with your cheeky grin
and a hint of your curls only visible,
never looking so lovely
or so fair.

I would like you to remember
how I wanted to steal you,
to keep you,
and never ever give you back . . . . .

■